The Road to

How Britain can leave the European Union

The case for unconditional, unilateral withdrawal

By

Gerard Batten MEP

Research by Pavel Stroilov

With a foreword by Professor Tim Congdon

"When in the Course of human events, it becomes necessary for one people to dissolve the political bands which have connected them with another, and to assume among the powers of the earth, the separate and equal station to which the Laws of Nature and of Nature's God entitle them, a decent respect to the opinions of mankind requires that they should declare the causes which impel them to the separation..."

US Declaration of Independence, 4th July 1776

Best Wishes,

27-9-2014

www.BretwaldaBooks.com
@Bretwaldabooks
bretwaldabooks.blogspot.co.uk/
Bretwalda Books on Facebook
First Published 2014

Bretwalda Books
Unit 8, Fir Tree Close, Epsom, Surrey KT17 3LD
info@BretwaldaBooks.com
www.BretwaldaBooks.com
ISBN 978-1-910440-02-5

Foreword:
Professor Tim Congdon

In 1944 Friedrich Hayek published his classic and most well-known work, The Road to Serfdom. Britain was then in the closing phases of the Second World War, an epic struggle to protect liberal democracy from fascism and totalitarianism. Hayek was anxious that social and political trends in Britain itself would undermine the free society, and warned against these trends. In 1946 an abridged version of The Road to Serfdom was published, with the frontispiece including a sentence from Sir Winston Churchill. To quote, "The essential aspects of democracy are the freedom of the individual within the framework of laws passed by Parliament, to order his life as he pleases, and the uniform enforcement of tribunals independent of the Executive."

Churchill's vision of Britain was clear and it remains familiar. All the same, it deserves restatement. Churchill saw Britain as a democracy characterised by the freedom of the individual under laws passed by its Parliament. What would he think about his country today? Dozens of so-called "competences", meaning areas of public policy-making, have been handed over to the European Commission for its determination. The Commission is a supranational bureaucracy indifferent to democratic approval or disapproval at the national level. Bureaucracy has replaced democracy, while the nation state of Britain has lost sovereignty and become subordinate to the jerry-built federal construction that is the European Union.

The UK's own Parliament has become a sideshow, even an anachronism, because true power lies with institutions located in other European countries. The European Commission promulgates not law in the usually understood sense, but

Directives and Regulations backed up by "Decisions". (Decisions are judgements from the Commission about the compliance of nations with Directives and Regulations.) Freedom of the individual under the law allows people to do whatever they wish, as long as they are not breaking the law. Directives and Regulations prescribe certain standards of conduct and behaviour, and enable the state to require people to act in ways that its functionaries deem good and worthwhile.

Much has gone wrong – horribly wrong – with the government of Britain since the Second World War. Undoubtedly, a key turning –point was the application to join the then European Economic Community (or "Common Market") in 1972. It was this step that led to EEC and eventually EU membership. Over time that resulted in the wholesale transfer of sovereignty to EU institutions by means of a series of treaties (the Single European Act of 1986, the Maastricht Treaty of 1992, the Amsterdam Treaty of 1997, the Nice Treaty of 2001) that culminated in the Lisbon Treaty of 2009. Britain's long-run constitutional arrangements, including those "essential aspects of democracy" applauded by Churchill, can be recovered only if Britain leaves the EU.

In Thier The Road to Freedom Gerard Batten explains how Britain can restore liberty and democracy to our country. Their work distinguishes Britain's legal and constitutional traditions from those of its European neighbours, and provides a road-map for the UK to leave the EU and to regain those traditions. It is well-written, powerfully argued and thoroughly topical. I commend it without reservation as a vital contribution to the most important political debate in Britain today.

CONTENTS

1. Introduction..06

2. The Article 50 trap..09

    2.1. European Communities vs. Free Trade: a forgotten battle.......... 13

    2.2. EEA and the 'Norwegian model'..16

    2.3. The 'Swiss model'..18

    2.4. GSP (Generalised Scheme of Preferences) and 'GSP Plus'.............21

    2.5. A new model? 21

    2.6. Independence in practice and in principle.......................23

3. The problem of 'vested rights'..25

    3.1. The lesson from Greenland's withdrawal.........................25

    3.2. 'Vested rights' and EU immigration...............................26

    3.3. What are the limits of 'vested rights'?............................29

    3.4. 'Vested rights' other than immigration............................32

4. The legal basis of unconditional withdrawal....................34

    4.1. Under our Constitution...34

    4.2. Under international law..38

    4.3. Anschluss Null und Nichtig (Union Null and Void).............39

5. Historic precedents 41

    5.1. Collapse of the Soviet Union..41

    5.2. EU Treaties: honoured more in breach than in observance..........45

6. The exit plan..47

    6.1. The Economy and trade...47

    6.2. Justice and Home Affairs..51

    6.3. Immigration..55

    6.4. The Environment..58

    6.5. Defence and Foreign Affairs..59

7. The transitional period..61

    7.1. Repeal of the European Communities Act.......................64

    7.2. Negotiations after the withdrawal.................................64

    7.3. What happens to the acquis communitaire? 66

    7.4. Directives and Decisions..67

8. Conclusion...69

Appendix: 'GSP Plus' list of international conventions....................72

About the Author...74

1. Introduction

The great EU project is now nearing its final phase. We are close to seeing the creation of a United States of Europe, in fact if not yet in name. Intrinsically inefficient and wasteful, the EU has helped to bring a number of its member states' economies to their knees. The economies of all its member states have suffered because of the dead hand of its bureaucracy, and never-ending regulation on business; and those member states rash enough to join the European Single Currency (bar Germany) are hardest hit of all. If Britain does not take decisive action to disengage itself from the failed experiment of European political and economic integration we may well find ourselves buried in its ruins.

As the real purpose of the European Union becomes apparent to all who have eyes to see, the harder it is for its proponents in Britain to disguise its true nature. The Europhiles have to rely on scare stories about the impossibility of life outside the EU rather than promote its benefits, of which there are none, at least none that could not be equally enjoyed outside.

So it is hardly surprising that the British public is now increasingly making up its mind that Britain would indeed be better off outside the EU. Those people who really believe in the EU are becoming thin on the ground. Nick Clegg, Leader of the Liberal Democrats boldly put his Party forward as "the Party of in" in the European elections of May 2014, only to find that as a consequence his Members of the European Parliament became the MEPs of 'out' – out of their jobs that is.

Mr Clegg has been wrongly criticised for espousing what his Party believes in. This he did; it was merely that the electorate did not want it, and eleven of his twelve MEPs lost their seats. That is what democracy is supposed to be about: parties put their case to the electors; if the voters want it, they vote for it, and if they don't want it they vote for an alternative party. The alternative in this case was the UK Independence Party with its unequivocal policy of EU withdrawal - and it topped the vote.

The increasing tide of voter antipathy to the EU, and the UKIP electoral threat, has caused David Cameron to offer a phoney referendum; but what is on offer is merely a re-run of Harold Wilson's referendum of 1975, except this time in slow motion. If the British electorate gives Mr Cameron a majority, he promises to 'renegotiate' our terms of membership, and then put it to an 'in-out' referendum. Of course, this time around it is supposed to be a 'real' cast-iron guarantee; and of course he has said that he will recommend acceptance of whatever terms he has negotiated.

Even if you believe this hog-wash, what if there actually is a referendum, and what if the British public vote to leave? Are we really supposed to believe that the EU will allow us to exit in an orderly fashion? Over six decades the EU has engineered the surrender of 28 nation states' sovereignty by means of lies, deceit and manipulation. They have no intention of allowing Britain to leave. After all, the EU has an impressive record of wriggling out of previous referendum results.

When Parliament finally resolves to withdraw, the EU and its quislings will try to make that withdrawal purely formal, and to keep us EU members, in fact if not in name. After all, they are the ones who make the rules. The rule they have made on the procedure for withdrawal is Article 50 of the Lisbon Treaty - and it is a trap.

The European Union's process of 'ever closer union' is fashioned like the jaws of a shark. The teeth slant backwards. Once inside the mouth the only route is onwards down the gullet to digestion. Membership of the EU has been deliberately constructed over six decades and six treaties in order to make exit from the EU near impossible. It is a Gordian Knot of a problem that requires an Alexandrian solution.

Article 50 is designed to put the EU in a strong position to pressurise the would-be, leaving nation into accepting their terms of exit. This detrimental dog's breakfast is hardly likely to be what the electorate have in mind when they vote in a referendum to leave the EU. Once the decision has been made then it is better to deliver the Alexandrian blow rather than endlessly fiddle with the strands.

2. The Article 50 Trap

Prior to the Lisbon Treaty there was no mechanism for any country to leave the EU. From the EU's viewpoint, that was actually a threat since any country wishing to do so merely had to invoke their sovereign right to tear up the Treaty and walk away. They realised that growing discontent with the EU, and the growing anti-EU vote in Britain, meant they needed to construct a mechanism for preventing a country leaving. That mechanism is Article 50 of the Lisbon Treaty.

Article 50 provides a procedure for a 'negotiated withdrawal' of any member-state. In theory it takes two years, but that period may be prolonged. Throughout that period, we remain bound by all the EU Treaties, Regulations and Directives, etc.; but at the same time we are excluded from all the EU Council discussions about the terms of our withdrawal. In the end, the EU and its former member-state are supposed to conclude a 'withdrawal agreement' on their future relationship.

Article 50 of the Lisbon Treaty:

1.   Any Member State may decide to withdraw from the Union in accordance with its own constitutional requirements.

2.   A Member State which decides to withdraw shall notify the European Council of its intention. In the light of the guidelines provided by the European Council, the Union shall negotiate and conclude an agreement with that State, setting out the arrangements for its withdrawal, taking account of the framework for its future relationship with the Union. That agreement shall be negotiated in

---

accordance with Article 218(3) of the Treaty on the Functioning of the European Union. It shall be concluded on behalf of the Union by the Council, acting by a qualified majority, after obtaining the consent of the European Parliament.

3.   The Treaties shall cease to apply to the State in question from the date of entry into force of the withdrawal agreement or, failing that, two years after the notification referred to in paragraph 2, unless the European Council, in agreement with the Member State concerned, unanimously decides to extend this period.

4.   For the purposes of paragraphs 2 and 3, the member of the European Council or of the Council representing the withdrawing Member State shall not participate in the discussions of the European Council or Council or in decisions concerning it.

A qualified majority shall be defined in accordance with Article 238(3)(b) of the Treaty on the Functioning of the European Union.

5.   If a State which has withdrawn from the Union asks to rejoin, its request shall be subject to the procedure referred to in Article 49.

A number of deep and irreparable flaws are apparent even on the face of this article. Let's imagine, for the sake of argument, that the Tories have won a general election and have somehow been forced to keep their promise to hold a referendum on leaving the EU: the country votes to leave; and yet, that in itself does not take us out of the EU. Instead, we are told there is a special procedure to follow. The government then "notifies the European Council" according to paragraph 2; and that starts another 'renegotiation' of our "future relationship with the Union".

In theory, it is supposed to take two years; however, the UK government and the European Council can agree to extend that period, again and again, indefinitely if they decide, without any further referendum.

An eminent German lawyer, Dr Jochum Herbst, wrote a detailed legal analysis of Article 50 (which was at that point was still known as Article I-60 of the European Constitution) and what the process of withdrawal might look like in practice; he concluded: *"Bearing the complexity of these issues in mind, I am convinced that the two-year notice period, as a general rule, is far too short for negotiating and concluding a withdrawal implementation agreement in an "average" Member State withdrawal case".* [1] So if they want a plausible excuse to prolong the renegotiations from 2 years to, say, 10, they will have no difficulty in finding any number of them.

Many of those people will, no doubt, enjoy the process. It is likely to create quite a few comfortable jobs both in Brussels and in Westminster. So, it may well be that the process of withdrawal will simply never end – at least not before the ultimate collapse of the entire EU project.

Throughout that period, we will still be bound by EU Treaties in accordance with paragraph 3; and by virtue of EU Treaties, we will also be bound by all the EU Regulations and Directives. We will remain inside the EU for all intents and purposes, except that we will be excluded from the EU discussions concerning our future, in accordance with paragraph 4.

That is the mechanics, unsatisfactory as they are; but now imagine the politics. For two solid years (or much longer) we will have the BBC, elements of the press, the metropolitan political class, and possibly the President of the United States, to name just a few, telling us that we cannot survive outside of the EU. They

---

[1] *Jochum Herbst, "Observations on the Right to Withdraw from the European Union: Who are the 'Masters of the Treaties'?", German Law Journal (6:2005), p1755*

will take every opportunity to scaremonger the British public into believing that EU exit will result on loss of trade, loss of jobs, and calamities of all sorts.

How would a Prime Minister hold his nerve under this kind of fire, especially one who does not believe in exit in any case? How do we know he and the EU would not simply keep 'negotiating' until and unless they think it safe to hold another referendum to overrule the first one? After all, this is what EU referendums are like historically: A 'Yes' vote is final. A 'No' vote means you have to try again and again until there is the 'right' result.

So it will only be called a withdrawal; in reality it is just another name for Cameron's 'renegotiation'. It is being sold to us like a shining path to regaining our independence: just let David Cameron try to 'renegotiate' with the EU just once more; if we don't like the result, we can vote to leave the EU in 2017, and then… there is more 'renegotiation', perhaps forever – with Britain as a supplicant seeking permission and terms for regaining her independence and self-determination.

Let us assume however, that at some point in the future that process comes to an end. The European Council, with the obvious benefit of having excluded us from its discussions, comes up with some agreement on the UK's "future relationship with the Union", and our government agrees. The phrase "our future relationship with the EU" rightly provokes instant suspicion: whenever it was used in the past it simply meant doing what we are told by Brussels. Realistically, what might that "withdrawal agreement" look like?

First of all, like any international agreement, it may set any date, however remote, for its coming into force. It may provide for a transitional period of any length, throughout which we would still be bound by EU law and perhaps some additional onerous conditions.

But even if it ever comes to an actual withdrawal, it will not be an unconditional withdrawal. It will not be a full restoration of national independence. It will probably provide for some form of semi-independence, along the same lines of Switzerland's or Norway's present relationships with the EU. Therefore, the peculiar and tragic situation of those two nations vis-à-vis the European Union merit a detailed consideration; but before exploring that, we have to understand the organisation known as **'European Economic Area' (EEA)**.

2.1. European Communities vs. Free Trade: a forgotten battle

One of the lies we are repeatedly told about modern European history is that there was no real alternative to the European Community, which later mutated into the European Union: it was only natural for West European democracies to have free-trade between themselves, and the EEC was initially supposed to be no more than a Common Market.

In reality, not one, but two rival trade blocs gradually emerged in the post-war Western Europe. In 1957, 'the inner six' (Belgium, France, Germany, Italy, Luxembourg and the Netherlands) founded the **European Economic Community (EEC)**, which eventually became the European Union. In 1960, 'the outer seven' (Austria, Denmark, Norway, Portugal, Sweden, Switzerland, and the UK) founded the **European Free Trade Association** (EFTA).

Not only were the EEC and EFTA rival trade blocs; they pursued rather different ideals. EFTA, with the United Kingdom as its largest economy and political leader, was founded upon a belief in free-trade, not only within the organisation, but also with the rest of the world. Having abolished the trade barriers between themselves, each country was also free to have its own trade agreements with the outer world.

The EEC, by contrast, was destined to a gradual integration into a single political state, a customs union was merely the first step; declarations about free-trade were mere propaganda. It never abolished trade barriers with the outer world; instead,

13

centralised political structures were created right away, and the trade policies of the 'inner six' taken over from the national governments by the European Commission. In the course of its history and to the present day, its trade policy in many areas was often protectionist; and in one area, agriculture, its protectionism was institutionalised in the 'Common Agricultural Policy'.

The EEC won over EFTA when Edward Heath took Britain into the EEC without a democratic mandate but by means a narrow Parliamentary majority conspiratorially achieved by secret back room deals with Labour and Liberal MPs. Not only was that arguably treason but was also a betrayal of our allies in Europe, and of our common ideal of genuine free trade. Once the UK had 'defected' to the EEC, smaller EFTA economies followed suit, with the exception of Switzerland and Norway, where referendums said 'No' to capitulation (see below). By now, EFTA has four members: Norway, Switzerland, Iceland and Lichtenstein.

Meanwhile, the growing European Community was struggling with the classic imperial dilemma. On one hand, its whole idea was a gradual abolition of the nation-state and integration into a single state; but as often happens with utopian ideas, this is easier said than done, and the greater the number of nations, the more problems there are in melding them into one. On the other hand, like every empire, the EEC/EU needs to expand, absorbing more and more nations, and therefore causing itself more and more problems.

To that classic imperial problem, two French socialists, Francois Mitterrand and Jaques Delors, proposed a classic imperial solution. A United Europe was to be organised in what they called "concentric circles". The EU would merely be the innermost circle, and even there, some countries would be more equal than others. But there would also be outer circles, outside the EU but within its sphere of influence, consisting of those as yet unworthy or unwilling to become full members.

The second 'concentric circle', right next to the EU, was blueprinted by Delors as the 'European Economic Space', but then renamed the '**European Economic Area (EEA)**'. The EEA became primarily the mechanism for the governance of the defeated EFTA countries before they finally join the EU. The original idea was that the EEA would be governed directly by the European Commission and the European Court of Justice (ECJ); however, the legal opinion of ECJ judges was that such an arrangement would violate the EU's own treaties.

The solution eventually found was to set up an organisation called the **EFTA Surveillance Authority**, put it in Brussels next door to the European Commission, and task it with conveying the Commission's will to the EFTA countries. Similarly, they set up the EFTA Court, and put it next door to the European Court of Justice in Luxembourg. It is interesting to note that neither Belgium nor Luxembourg are, or have ever been, members of EFTA.[2]

While EFTA and EEA are nowadays often confused and the two terms used as synonyms, they are different organisations:

EFTA is the remnant of what was once an important trade bloc; first led and then betrayed by the UK. It only has four members: Iceland, Lichtenstein, Norway and Switzerland. None of them are formally members of the EU; and no country in history was ever simultaneously a member of both EC/EU and EFTA.

The **EEA** includes all the European Union member states, plus Iceland, Lichtenstein, and Norway. It is effectively the EU's mechanism for governing its semi-autonomous provinces. Symbolically, it is run from Brussels and Luxembourg, i. e. from outside EFTA and inside the EU.

---

[2] *On the detailed history of negotiations and proceedings leading to the establishment of the EEA judicial system, see: Leif Sevon. The EEA Judcial System and the Supreme Courts of the EFTA States. European Journal of International Law (1992) 329-340*

2.2. EEA and the 'Norwegian model'

Norway, one of the founding members of EFTA, negotiated its accession (defection) to the European Community at the same time as the UK – in the early 1970s. By 1972, the agreement was complete. The Norwegian political class, like ours, was overwhelmingly in favour of joining. The Norwegian Parliament, like ours, voted "Yes". Unlike us, the Norwegians were given a referendum, and the country voted 'No' by 53.5% to 46.5%. The government resigned. The new government concluded a bilateral trade treaty with the EEC.

Then there was another referendum in 1994, on the grounds that 22-year-old referendum result was too old to have sufficient democratic legitimacy. Norway again voted 'No' to EU membership, 52.2% to 47.8%. By now however, the political class knew better than just to implement the will of the people. They took Norway into the European Economic Area (EEA). The EEA was represented to the voters as an alternative to EU membership.

In reality, it was something more than that. As part of the EEA, Norway became an EU member for nearly all intents and purposes, and is subject to EU legislation and powers in the following areas:

- 'free movement of goods';
- 'free movement of services'
- 'free movement of capital'
- 'free movement of persons' (open door immigration for all EU citizens);
- Schengen Zone;
- Europol (the EU's own criminal intelligence agency);
- Frontex (EU border agency)
- European Defence Agency and EU Battlegroups
- Social Charter legislation
- Consumer protection
- Environment
- Company law

As an EEA member, Norway pays tribute to the EU (**EEA grants** and also the separate **Norway grants**). Because it is not an EU member, it does not receive any money back from the EU's 'policies and development funds'.

Norway's contributions to the EU is a clear example of taxation without representation. Norway is not represented in the European Parliament (not a big loss, admittedly, but still a fact). It is not represented in the Commission or the Council. In theory, it can veto the adoption of EU legislation through its representation in European Surveillance Agency. In practice, the EU always gets its way.

Norwegians describe their system as 'government by fax', since most of their legislation is received from Brussels. Perhaps that should now be updated to 'government by email'?

On the bright side, unlike full EU members, Norway has retained control of its own global trade. It benefits from EFTA's 32 free trade agreements with countries all over the world from Canada to Israel to China. It is free to enter its own free trade agreements and has done so. It is not bound by the Common Agricultural Policy; it is not bound by the Common Fisheries Policy; it is not bound by the European Arrest Warrant; to name just a few impositions.

To sum up, Norway enjoys some autonomy within the EU empire. It is certainly doing better than the UK, as a full EU member. And yet, it is not an independent country.

Two other EFTA member-states, Iceland and Lichtenstein, have also subscribed to EEA along the lines of the 'Norwegian model', with similar results.

If we do the same we would still be bound by **5,758** pieces of EU legislation, as compared to the overall **20,868** currently in force (although not all of them necessarily apply to Britain, e.g. for geographical reasons or because of some negotiated 'opt-outs').[3]

That would admittedly be an improvement – but not independence.

2.3. The 'Swiss model'

The story of Switzerland is, in a sense, different from Norway's; and the difference is solely due to a more democratic Swiss Constitution, where referenda are easier to initiate and therefore happen more often. As a consequence, in leading its people into EU captivity, the Swiss government had to get around more referenda results than is usual. The path has been more twisted, but the destination is the same.

In the 1992 referendum, Switzerland voted not just against EU membership, **but also against joining the EEA**. There is still an outstanding Swiss application to join the EU, but it is 'suspended' indefinitely. Despite the repeated referendum results, the Swiss government has not withdrawn that application. Moreover, full EU membership officially remained a 'strategic goal' of the Swiss foreign policy until 2006, when it was downgraded to 'an option'.

In the meantime, the Swiss government and the EU have negotiated over a hundred bilateral treaties and set up almost as many bilateral committees, with the result of Switzerland adopting most of the EU legislation without formally being an EU or EEA member. These include:

- Abolition of trade barriers;
- 'Free movement of people', i. e. open door immigration for EU citizens (resulting in **some 20% of the country's population now being immigrants from the EU**);
- Membership of Schengen Agreement, i. e. abolition of border controls;
- Large elements of EU law on 'police and criminal justice' (e.g. those under the Schengen acquis, including SIS ((Schengen Information System)) and SIRENE

---

[3] *As of December 2013: see Richard North, Flexcit: a definitive EU exit plan for Britain. p. 17*

    ((Supplementary Information Request at the National Entry)));
- Asylum;
- Taxation (Switzerland is no longer a tax heaven for EU residents);
- The European Environment Agency;
- Significant elements of the EU's Common Foreign and Security Policy (albeit on a case-by-case basis);
- An exchange rate mechanism ties the Swiss franc to the Euro;
- Switzerland pays contributions to the EU budget.

Because all new EU law under these and other headings comes to Switzerland through EU-Swiss bilateral committees, unlike EU member states, in theory Switzerland has preserved its right of veto. In practice, however, the choice is always the same as the EU member-states have: either do as you are told or withdraw altogether. Under the so-called Guillotine Clause, **if Switzerland vetoes any particular EU law, the EU can retaliate by cancelling nearly all its treaties with Switzerland.**

For example, in 2008 the EU demanded that Switzerland extends the 'free movement of people' to Bulgarians and Romanians; for whatever reason, the Swiss voters had their doubts about that. In some other country, that would not matter; but in Switzerland, that meant a referendum. The EU ambassador then publicly threatened that, in case of a 'No' result, the EU would cancel a whole raft of bilateral agreements with Switzerland within the next six months. In response, the Swiss government promised to do everything in its power to secure a 'Yes' vote – and so it did.

More recently, in February 2014, Switzerland voted at a referendum to effectively abolish 'free movement of people' with the EU, and re-introduce some form of immigration control. Contrary what one might assume, that had no immediate effect on Swiss immigration law: that only started a 3-year-long process of 'renegotiation' between the Swiss government and the EU (both of whom had strenuously opposed that initiative in the first place).

The moment the votes had been counted, the EU responded with pressure and threats of various economic sanctions, jeopardising Switzerland's access to the 'single market'; the Commission spokesman declared the whole matter was "non-negotiable". It remains to be seen whether Switzerland eventually gives in to the pressure; if not, it may well be on its way out of its 'bilateral' arrangement with the EU altogether. Many in Switzerland hope that in the next three years, Britain's withdrawal may undermine the EU's ability to pressurise them. It would be a pity if we let them down.

All this is not to say that the Swiss model is literally no better than a full membership of the EU. It is better. For instance, in 2006 the Swiss Federal Government commissioned a report which showed that full EU membership would cost up to six times more than their existing bilateral arrangements. An estimated 40 per cent of Swiss laws are made by the EU [4] , which – on one view of things – is considerably better than the figures we are used to seeing in the British debate, where the number is variously estimated as between 50% to 84%.

So, it is easy to see why Switzerland has preferred its 'bilateral' semi-independence to full EU membership. With the EU, as a general rule, any opt-out or wriggle-out makes things better. And yet, it is not independence; and in the fundamental sense of national sovereignty, Switzerland today is almost in the same position as Britain.

---

[4] *See Richard North, Flexcit: a definitive EU exit plan for Britain.p. 43*

2.4. GSP (Generalised Scheme of Preferences) and 'GSP Plus'

If we travel yet further from the 'formal' European Union across its outer 'concentric circles', the landscape remains rather unattractive for a very long time. In breach of World Trade Organisation principles, the EU has politicised its international trade under its so-called 'GSP Plus' scheme. 'GSP Plus' is different from GSP (Generalised Scheme of Preferences) which allows certain former colonies preferential trade treatment within the limits of WTO rules. By contrast, 'GSP Plus' employs further trade preferences as a political leverage, offering them only in exchange for ratification and implementation of no fewer than **27** international conventions.

Sixteen of these Conventions (see Appendix, List A) relate to "**core political, human and labour rights**", and include such controversial documents as the communist-inspired **International Covenant on Economic, Social and Cultural Rights**. The other 11 (list B) are the '**conventions relating to the environment, good governance and the fight against drug production and trafficking**'. Some of them are even more controversial, e.g. the **Kyoto Protocol**. Both lists are reproduced in full in **Appendix I**.

Fifteen non-EU countries have been admitted to join the 'GSP Plus' scheme on these conditions: Armenia, Azerbaijan, Bolivia, Colombia, Costa Rica, Ecuador, El Salvador, Georgia, Guatemala, Honduras, Mongolia, Nicaragua, Peru, Paraguay, and Panama.

2.5. A new model?

Iceland and Norway, Lichtenstein and Switzerland are all better off than any EU member-state; and yet, none of them is independent of the EU. They only have a greater autonomy than other parts of the same empire. EEA or Swiss-style bilateral agreements are part of the same maze of EU's 'opt-ins' and 'opt-outs' where we have been wandering, under the leadership of successive Tory and Labour governments, from one dead-end to another since 1972. This is not what we mean by withdrawal from the EU.

At the same time, the hypothetical 'withdrawal agreement' under Article 50 on our 'framework of future relationship with the EU' can only be yet another combination of 'opt-ins' and 'opt-outs'. Further below, we will consider the impact of our EU membership on different policy areas, and see that there are hardly any benefits we get from it.

Strictly speaking, a cost/benefit analysis of EU membership is impossible: it is all costs and virtually no benefits. Indeed, which bits of the EU is it in the national interest to preserve: open door immigration, the loss of our traditional freedoms and protections under the law, over-regulation on business, the Common Agricultural Policy? The list is endless. Nobody in their right mind would want to 'opt in to' any of those. But if we 'opt out' of all, what will be left? Why is a 'withdrawal agreement' necessary at all, unless it is a backdoor into some, or all, of these things?

It is of course obvious that **free trade** with Europe and the rest of the world is in the national interest of the UK. Contrary to what we are often told however, EU membership does not help that at all. It is in fact a major obstacle to trade. A lot of countries have free trade agreements with the EU without being members of the EU, or the EEA, or having to accept any of the EU law. Examples include the European micro-states Andorra, Monaco, and San Marino but also big economies like South Korea, Mexico, Israel and Turkey.

The experience of numerous countries over the past half a century shows this trend: the further you keep from the EU institutions, the better deal they offer you. **We must begin by reasserting our independence and establishing ourselves as an equal partner, and then we can have a genuine free-trade treaty.**

Anyone who has begun trying to construct the right combination of 'opt-ins' and 'opt-outs' has ended up with exactly what they had voted against when rejecting an EU membership. **A free trade deal should be a consequence of withdrawal and not a precondition**. In fact, as will be shown below, both for economic and for legal reasons, an unconditional withdrawal from the EU cannot seriously jeopardise our trade on that or any other market.

2.6. Independence in practice and in principle

Eternal vigilance is the price of liberty. The question of this country's independence was never simply a question of being signatories to one European treaty and not another. The threat to the British sovereignty did not begin with the present legal forms of the EU; nor does it end there. There are influential schools of political thought which believe that all nation-states such as ours belong to the dustbin of history. To quote the closing words of Jean Monnet's memoirs, *"The sovereign nations of the past can no longer solve the problems of the present: they cannot ensure their own progress or control their own future. And the Community itself is only a stage on the way to an organised world of tomorrow."* [5]

It is an old imperial trick to give a former dominion a formal independence, but still to tie it to the empire by leaving behind a puppet government, which would happily sign any number of onerous treaties on 'mutual' friendship and 'equal' partnership. Before we get too far away from the subject of Norway, it is pertinent to recall the name of Quisling and everything it stands for.

History shows that a country may be effectively occupied and annexed without any need to sign any treaties. Over the past 40 years, the Conservative, Lib-Dem and Labour parties have proven themselves to be EU quislings in this country. How can we trust them to negotiate the conditions of our withdrawal with the people they repeatedly betrayed us to? Is there any doubt they have much more in common with the Euro-fanatics than they have with us?

These two problems, the loss of our national independence and the corruption of our political elite, have always been closely interlinked. In the final analysis, it is one and the same problem. So long as we are governed by those who do not believe in the democratic nation state and national self-determination, such 'leaders' will always find someone to sell their country to.

This is the main reason why UKIP has never been, and must never be, a one-issue party prepared to sacrifice any other principle or policy to a victory on this one issue; prepared to sacrifice itself for anything labelled a withdrawal from the EU. We recognised that the EU is, at this particular point of our history, the greatest disaster brought on our heads by our cross-party 'political elite'. But this also implies that ultimately, the EU is only a symptom of a much deeper problem.

The problem of withdrawal might, perhaps, have looked different if we had a patriotic and trustworthy government. At least, such a government could have been trusted to protect our national interest in the negotiations with the EU. In other words, it could have been trusted to walk away from those negotiations as soon as they saw they were pointless and detrimental; and that would be fairly soon.

There is simply no objective case, from the national interest perspective, for negotiations under Article 50. It can only be advocated for political tactical reasons. This may or may not be clever tactics, but we must never sacrifice principles to tactics - or we will ultimately lose the possibility of regaining our national independence.

As it is, all we can do is to offer the country a credible alternative to the political class who have made the 'renegotiation' of a national disaster their permanent (and well-paid) job; and the only credible alternative is unconditional withdrawal.

---

[5] *Quoting from: Richard North, Flexcit: a definitive EU exit plan for Britain. P. 1*

3. The problem of 'Vested Rights'

3.1. The lesson from Greenland's withdrawal

Only one country has ever negotiated a withdrawal from what was then the Common Market: Greenland in 1985. Any comparison between that and the potential UK withdrawal would be so strained as to be practically useless: the population and economy of Greenland is about one thousandth of ours, and the Common Market in 1985 was very different from the European Union in 2014. And yet, some legal issues which emerged over Greenland's withdrawal in 1985 may give us an indication of the enormous problem Britain will face if we go down the Article 50 route.

To quote from the 1983 European Commission document (Status of Greenland: Commission opinion, COM (83) 66 final, 2 February 1983, p. 12):

Retention of vested rights

Provision should be made for appropriate measures to protect companies and persons who have exercised the right of establishment as well as Community workers employed in Greenland. The extremely small number of persons affected and the case-law of the Court of Justice that has already been established in favour of the retention of pension rights acquired by workers during periods of employment in a territory which has subsequently ceased to belong to the Community give no reason to suppose that there will be any major difficulties in this area, even if the future status of Greenland were to rule out the principle of free movement. It would, however, be preferable to retain the substance of the Community rules, at least in respect of Community workers employed in Greenland at the time of withdrawal.

Typically, the Commission's document did not opine at all about what should happen to 'vested rights' of Greenland's citizens who might be living or working elsewhere in the Common Market. Eventually, the 1985 Greenland Treaty simply left the matter to the EEC Council – Article 2 of the Protocol on special arrangements for Greenland provided:

The Commission shall make proposals to the Council, which shall act by a qualified majority, for the transitional measures which it considers necessary, by reason of the entry into force of the new arrangements, with regard to the maintenance of rights acquired by natural or legal persons during the period when Greenland was part of the Community and the regularization of the situation with regard to financial assistance granted by the Community to Greenland during that period.

3.2. 'Vested Rights' and EU immigration

In the case of Greenland this problem only affected an "extremely small number of persons". **In the case of Britain, it will affect hundreds of thousands of people, if not millions.**

As the House of Commons research paper [6] explains:

*Many provisions of EU law create individual rights which are directly enforceable in national courts (either horizontally between private individuals, or vertically by an individual against the state). These cover areas such as **free movement of workers,** free movement of goods and freedom of establishment. **If any EU rights can be enforced after withdrawal, it is likely to include these.***
[Emphasis added]

Under the EU Treaties, we owe countless legal obligations not merely to 27 foreign states, but also to 500 million 'EU citizens'.

In strict legal terms, if we want a withdrawal in accordance with EU Treaties, it is from each and every EU citizen that we now need a 'divorce'- amicable or otherwise. As the European Court of Justice put it as long ago as in 1963 in the case of **van Gend & Loos:**

"the Community constitutes a new legal order [...] the subjects of which comprise not only Member States but also their nationals. [...] Independently of the legislation of Member States, community law [...] not only imposes obligations on individuals but also intended to confer upon them rights which become part of their legal heritage." [7]

This doctrine may be controversial in England; it is completely non-controversial in Europe. This doctrine is firmly enshrined in the subsequent ECJ case-law and in the EU Treaties, most manifestly as the concept of EU Citizenship. The EU Council, which would be in charge of negotiating the 'withdrawal agreement', would have a legal obligation to protect the 'vested rights' of all 'EU citizens'. The EU Council is legally obliged to insist on that as part of the 'withdrawal agreement', and will be in breach of EU law if it accepts a different one.

From their point of view, this issue is non-negotiable. Ultimately, this probably means that if we want an 'amicable divorce' and a 'withdrawal agreement', we have to accept 'free movement of people', just like Norway and Switzerland did. After all, the fundamental premise of any negotiations under Article 50 would be that 'free movement of people' is **law**; and therefore, it cannot be changed retrospectively to the detriment of EU citizens.

It would be argued that millions of EU immigrants who have already exercised their right to come to the UK under the EU Treaties can no longer be deprived of that right. It would

---

[6] *P. 14*

[7] *Case C-26/62, van Gend & Loos, 1963 E.C.R. 1.*

be pointed out, correctly, that if we try to do so, any of the EU immigrants in the UK could successfully take us to the European Court of Justice; that the ECJ would certainly accept jurisdiction (on the basis that the 'vested rights' include the right to sue us in ECJ) and certainly rule against us.

Alternatively, if we join EFTA and the EEA, they can take us to the EFTA Court (which is but a shadow of the ECJ). Yet alternatively, the EFTA Surveillance Authority could take us to the EFTA Court. Of course, we would be able to defy and ignore the judgements of either court; but if we have to do that in the end anyway, there is no reason why we should not withdraw unilaterally in the first place. Moreover, if we retain any part of the 'EU law' as part of our law, it is quite likely that our own courts will recognise the doctrine of 'vested rights'. Since these rights were recognised in the English law at the time the EU immigrants took advantage of them; the Common Law will presume their residence in the UK to be lawful despite the country's subsequent withdrawal from the EU.

Under the EU Treaties, there is simply no lawful way to abolish or invalidate those rights. Under our Constitution, there is one lawful way, and one only, and that is by an Act of Parliament. It will have to declare and enact that the immigration rights arising out of EU Treaties have been void throughout; and then provide for the legal basis on which such persons can remain in the country, or not, as the case may be.

So, even if, by whatever miracle, we persuade the EU Council to breach its legal duties and accept a withdrawal agreement without a 'free movement of people', that would not be the end of the story. We would then face years of legal battles fought against the EU under its own rules, and with its own politicised courts having the final say. They will have an overwhelming case against us under EU law, which we could only counter by challenging the legality of our EU membership in the first place. If we shall have to do that anyway, it is best to do it first, in our own Parliament and in our own courts.

No doubt, the future of millions of EU immigrants in the UK is an enormously difficult problem. Nobody is suggesting that our withdrawal from the EU should turn them into illegal immigrants overnight; some robust but humane transitional arrangements will be necessary. I propose what they might include further on; but this question, difficult as it is, is for the UK alone to decide. It is the EU's control of our immigration policy that has created this problem in the first place.

Some may say that 'free movement of people' is a price worth paying for the 'amicability' of our 'divorce' from the EU. Some may say, if it is good enough for Norway and Switzerland, it is good enough for us; but control of our borders and our immigration policy is one of the most important reasons why restoration of our sovereignty is so urgent. Whatever we do about it, we should of course treat EU immigrants already in this country fairly and reasonably; but one thing we cannot recognise is their continuing **right** to be here as part of their '**legal heritage**' as EU citizens.

3.3. What are the limits of 'vested rights'?

As we have seen above, the doctrine of 'vested rights' was inherent in the EEC project from a very early stage. However, the formal introduction of 'EU citizenship' in the Treaty on European Union (Maastricht) began a new era, where that doctrine was very significantly expanded and strengthened. A much more recent decision of the European Court of Justice which illustrates that is the case of *Ruiz Zambrano* (2011) C-34/09.

Mr. and Mrs. Zambrano were Colombian nationals who unsuccessfully claimed asylum in Belgium. While their asylum claim slowly progressed through the Belgian system of appeals, they had two children. Under the then Belgian law, it was possible to acquire Belgian citizenship for their children by virtue of the fact that they were born on Belgian soil. Their parents did so, and of course, by becoming Belgian citizens these children automatically became EU citizens as well. Their parents then re-applied for Belgian residence on the basis of being parents of Belgian citizens.

Meanwhile Mr Zambrano was working illegally for a Belgian company. Eventually, that was discovered by the authorities, he lost his job, and applied for unemployment benefit. That was refused: he would only be entitled to benefits after being in lawful employment for at least 468 days, and his employment had been unlawful. The Belgian Court referred the case to the European Court of Justice, which then held that:

1.   as EU citizens, Mr Zambrano's children had a right under the EU Treaties to reside in Belgium (or any other EU member-state);

2.   as EU citizens, those children were further entitled to a number of other rights, including in particular all those guaranteed by the EU's Charter of Fundamental Rights;

3.   the children would not be able to enjoy (a) their right to residence in Belgium and (b) their right to respect for their family life under the Charter of Fundamental Rights unless their parents were also allowed to live and work in Belgium;

4.   consequently, Mr. Zambrano should have been granted a work permit; therefore his former employment was lawful under the EU law; therefore he was now entitled to an unemployment benefit.

Not only the Belgian government, but also the governments of Denmark, Germany, Ireland, Greece, the Netherlands, Austria and Poland, as well as the European Commission, all opposed that argument as intervening parties before the European Court of Justice.

Much of the judgement, and particularly the more detailed underlying 'opinion' of the EU Advocate General (Eleanor Sharpston QC), is devoted to the legal distinction between the right to a 'free movement of people' in the EU on one hand, and the EU citizenship on the other.

The *'free movement of people'* means only that any national of one EU member-state is entitled to move to, and then reside in, in any other member-state. The EU law only comes into play **after** that person takes advantage of the EU Treaty to go from one member-state to another, it is only then that his right becomes 'vested'. On this basis, which was recognised in EU law before Maastricht, EU law would be of no avail to Mr Zambrano and his family.

But EU *citizenship* is different; by design, it is "*destined to become the fundamental status of nationals of the member states*"; and all sorts of rights and obligations are inherent in that status. It no longer matters whether an EU citizen has 'executed' his right to a 'free movement': the EU law protects his rights anyway, against his own or any other member state.

Let us consider the implications of that principle for the problem of UK's withdrawal from the EU. Not only will the existing EU immigrants preserve their 'vested right' to stay in the UK; if that principle is applied consistently, all EU citizens born before our withdrawal with have their right to come and live in the UK already vested in them, simply by virtue of their citizenship. If we continue to recognise EU law as law, we will probably have no power to take that right away from them.

The likeliest outcome is that, unable to square this circle, the government would simply accept a withdrawal agreement which preserves the right to 'free movement' of EU citizens into the UK indefinitely, on a similar basis to Norway. If you accept that our withdrawal may be conditional upon anything at all, this will be among the very first conditions which will be forced upon us.

3.4. 'Vested Rights' other than immigration

Immigration is the most obvious practical reason why recognition of 'vested rights' in a 'withdrawal agreement' in unacceptable to us, while anything other than that is unacceptable to the European Union. However, that is not the only reason. Almost half a century of being governed by the EU law has left similar 'legal heritage' in many other areas.

For example, the EU employment regulations under the so-called 'Social Chapter' are estimated to cost British economy between 2 and 2.5% of the GDP = approximately £32 bn. to £40 bn. per annum. [8] In a 2013 Sky News poll asking what powers the voters wanted to be 'repatriated' from the EU most urgently, employment law was named by 40% of the voters, third place at the top of the list after immigration and criminal justice, and ahead of the Common Agricultural and Fisheries Policies. In short, the regulatory burden of EU legislation is unbearable for our businesses, and is viewed as one of the top reasons why we should withdraw from the EU.

And yet, under the doctrine of 'vested rights', we would not be able to lighten that burden for many years, if not decades. Abolition of the 'Social Chapter' would have no retrospective effect. Anyone who had been employed under the old EU regulations will be able to rely on them in a lawsuit against the employer. Even if many of those lawsuits will ultimately fail, which is by no means certain, the very risk of costly legal actions would have the same stifling effect on businesses, especially small businesses. Formally out of the EU, we will still be left with the EU regulatory burden, and its immense cost on the economy for another generation.

---

[8] *Tim Congdon. How much does the European Union cost Britain? 2013 ed., p.p. 19-21.*

Another example is the European Convention of Human Rights, which is now incorporated into EU law as well as into our own Human Rights Act 1998. The Human Rights Act 1998 should be repealed, and we hardly want any 'vested' rights to be immune from the effects of such a repeal. Yet, that consequence would be inevitable if we accept this principle of EU law. Under the English Constitution, Parliament can legislate retrospectively; but to do so, it needs first to restore its own supremacy over the EU.

All sorts of things are nowadays construed as 'rights'. It may well be argued, with or without success in the Courts, that the purpose of the EU's environmental regulations (which cost the British economy at least 1.75% of the GDP, or some £28 bn. p. a. [9]) is to protect 'environmental rights' of EU citizens, that those rights have become 'vested' after those citizens lived under those regulations for some time, and therefore cannot be affected by our withdrawal from the EU.

By its very nature, any legal system creates all sorts of 'rights', and largely consists of various 'rights'. The EU legal system is no exception, and if we want to abolish it and to return to our own English system, we have to abolish it with all its rights and wrongs. No solution is possible within that system - it has to be declared null and void in the first place.

It follows that if we want a genuine withdrawal and not another 'opt out', we cannot negotiate with the EU Council as to which parts of 'EU law' we should preserve. We have to abolish it unreservedly and completely, down to the last jot and tittle; we have to reject and denounce it down to its most fundamental principles. **The only real way to do that is a unilateral and unconditional withdrawal.**

---

[9] *P.p. 18-19*

4. The legal basis of unconditional withdrawal

4.1. Under our Constitution

Various treaties concluded by the Crown with foreign sovereigns are often referred to as 'international law'. In many contexts, this is a convenient metaphor. In many ways, international treaties are indeed akin to the law. But in strict legal terms, they are not law, and for our present purposes, it is very important to clear any confusion about that.

In common with the majority of developed democracies, the United Kingdom is a 'dualist jurisdiction'. This means that our international treaties are, as such, a completely separate matter from our law. International treaties do not become part of our law unless expressly 'incorporated' by an Act of Parliament. Traditionally that principle has been considered as an important safeguard of democracy, and of democratic separation of powers. Like the rest of foreign policy, international treaties are made by the Executive; while the law can only be made or changed by the Legislature. Neither of these branches can be allowed to usurp the functions of the other.

As the House of Lords judgement in the case of Rayner v Department of Trade and Industry [1990] 2 AC 418 explains:

The Government may negotiate, conclude, construe, observe, breach, repudiate or terminate a treaty. Parliament may alter the laws of the United Kingdom. The courts must enforce those laws; judges have no power to grant specific performance of a treaty or to award damages against a sovereign state for breach of a treaty or to invent laws or misconstrue legislation in order to enforce a treaty.

A treaty is a contract between the governments of two or more sovereign states. International law regulates the relations between sovereign states and determines the validity, the interpretation and the enforcement of treaties. **A treaty to which Her Majesty's Government is a party does not alter the laws of the United Kingdom by means of legislation.** *Except to the extent that a treaty becomes incorporated into the laws of the United Kingdom by statute, the courts of the United Kingdom have no power to enforce treaty rights and obligations at the behest of a sovereign government or at the behest of a private individual.* [Emphasis added]

The Courts have consistently applied this principle to all sorts of international treaties, including of course the EEC/EU Treaties. After the government signed the Treaty of Rome in 1972, Norris McWhirter challenged that decision in Court as a breach of the Bill of Rights 1689 (*McWhirter v Attorney-General* [1972] C.M.L.R. 882). Lord Denning, Master of the Rolls, held in the Court of Appeal:

"Even though the Treaty of Rome has been signed, it has no effect, so far as these Courts are concerned, until it is made an Act of Parliament. Once it is implemented by an Act of Parliament, these Courts must go by the Act of Parliament. Until that day comes, we take no notice of it. I would recall what Lord Atkin said in Attorney-General for Canada v. Attorney-General for Ontario:

'... the stipulations of a treaty duly ratified do not within the Empire, by virtue of the treaty alone, have the force of law. If the national executive, the government of the day, decide to incur the obligations of a treaty which involve alteration of law they have to run the risk of obtaining the assent of Parliament to the necessary statute or statutes'."

Lord Justice Phillimore agreed, and added that the Treaty of Brussels (on UK's accession to the EC treaties) *"is to be ratified by the end of this year and to enter into force on 1 January 1973. Whether it is ratified or not depends, so far as this country is concerned, upon the present Bill before Parliament; it is that Bill which will or will not alter the law of this country; and unless and until that Bill becomes law this Court is not concerned with the provisions of the Treaty of Brussels."*

Therefore, what makes the EU Treaties part of our law is the European Communities Act 1972 alone. It is the statute which 'incorporates' all those treaties and all "rights, powers, liabilities, obligations and restrictions" arising out of EU law into the UK law.

It follows that, whatever a treaty may say about withdrawal, Parliament can always remove that treaty from the body of our domestic law simply **by repealing the European Economic Communities Act 1972.** From that moment the treaty becomes a purely foreign affair affecting nobody in this country except the Foreign Office.

While 'EU law' is recognised as part of English law, this is so only by force of the provisions of the European Communities Act 1972. 'EU law' is what constitutional lawyers call 'subordinate' or 'secondary' legislation. All EU Treaties, and the entire *acquis communitaire*, all 120,000 pages of it, hang on the single peg of the EEC Act 1972. Remove it, and all EU Treaties fall into the abyss of legal irrelevance, and the rest of the 'EU law' falls with them.

It is by the authority of Parliament, and Parliament alone, that 'EU law' is incorporated into our law. It follows that Parliament has the legal right to reverse that incorporation by repealing the 1972 Act at any time. Under the terms of the English Constitution, the Sovereign Queen in Parliament has every right to withdraw from the EU unilaterally at any time.

No constitutional lawyer in this country would argue otherwise, because that argument has already been tested before the High Court and failed. That was in the infamous case of the *Metric Martyrs*: the persecution of English market traders for selling vegetables by pounds and not by kilograms. The prosecution was represented by Eleanor Sharpston QC, that very barrister who later rose to become the Advocate-General of the EU Court of Justice in Luxembourg - perhaps the most influential legal post in Europe.

In her case against the Metric Martyrs, Miss Sharpston argued, among other things, that the supremacy of EU law over English law was (to quote from the judgement, para 56) *"subject only... to the possibility of withdrawal from the EU by express repeal of the 1972 [EEC] Act. And, if that were to be contemplated, **Parliament's hand would not be free. There would have to be consultations and negotiations first."***

However this argument was rejected by the High Court when Lord Justice Laws (with whom Mr. Justice Crane agreed) ruled:

Since we are dealing here with the strict legal position, and not with the realpolitik of the thing, I am not entirely sure why Miss Sharpston does not go the further mile and submit that Parliament could not legislate tomorrow to withdraw from the EU at all. Such a state of affairs might be said to be vouchsafed by the reasoning [of the European Court of Justice] in Costa v ENEL ("permanent limitation of their sovereign rights") [...] At all events, her argument appears to me to entail the proposition that the legislative and judicial institutions of the EU may set limits to the power of Parliament to make laws which regulate the legal relationship between the EU and the United Kingdom.

Thus baldly stated, that proposition is in my judgment false. [...] Parliament cannot bind its successors by stipulating against repeal, wholly or partly, of the 1972 Act. It cannot stipulate as to the manner and form of any subsequent legislation. [...] Thus there is nothing in the 1972 Act which allows the Court of Justice, or any other institutions of the EU, to touch or qualify the conditions of Parliament's legislative supremacy in the United Kingdom. Not because the legislature chose not to allow it; because by our law it could not allow it.

That being so, the legislative and judicial institutions of the EU cannot intrude upon those conditions. The British Parliament has not the authority to authorise any such thing. Being sovereign, it cannot abandon its sovereignty.

As a matter of constitutional law, the Queen in Parliament remains sovereign in this country. In 1972 Parliament legislated to make all EU law binding in the UK. Tomorrow it can legislate to repeal all EU law as far as the UK is concerned. Like any other Act of Parliament, it will be the law of the land. It cannot be against the law, that suggestion is nonsense. No English lawyer will ever argue against express words of a statute.

4.2. Under international law

Furthermore, Article 50 of the EU Treaty does not bind us in international law either. It has been persuasively argued on behalf of the Metric Martyrs, that under a correct interpretation of the **Vienna Convention on the Law of Treaties**, no provision of an international treaty can override a fundamental constitutional principle of national law; moreover all treaty partners are presumed to be aware of each other's constitutional principles. Parliamentary sovereignty in the UK is one such principle, and it cannot give way to any treaty provision. Constitutionally, it was Parliament itself that limited its rights by passing the EEC Act 1972 and delegated those rights to Brussels, but it retained the power to take those rights back at any time.

Further, **the right to national self-determination** is one of the first principles of international law, see the **Atlantic Charter**, the UN Charter, the **International Covenant on Civil and Political Rights**, etc. In international law there is no end of precedents of unilateral declarations of independence: from the American Revolution to the collapse of the USSR.

While all such declarations technically breached the imperial law, similar to Article 50 TEU, not only are they considered compatible with the international law, they form the very basis of international law as we know it. International law is based on the interaction of sovereign nations, many of whom derive their legal personality precisely from unilateral declarations of independence.

4.3. Anschluss Null und Nichtig (Union Null and Void)

At the end of the Second World War, the Allies liberated Austria and established a provisional government. The first thing that provisional government did was to declare that the country's Union with Germany had been unlawful and void from day one: '*Anschluss Null und Nichtig*' - 'Union null and void'.

Throughout the political history of the world, much of which has been a history of unions and disunions, that was always the 'cleanest' way to repudiate a union and restore national independence. Some other historical examples are considered further below. If there are legal grounds to declare our own Anschluss with the EU to be '*null und nichtig*' (it may be better to say that in German, to make sure nothing is lost in translation and the EU understands us correctly) that is certainly the right way to do that.

There is, of course, no problem in finding the legal grounds. Our EU membership has been unconstitutional in the first place, and arguably, void from day one. We have explored the issue in some depth in our book *Inglorious Revolution*; for present purposes, a short summary shall suffice:

•   A fundamental principle of the English Constitution is that '*no Parliament can bind its successors*'; yet the EEC Act 1973 purports to bind future Parliaments to legislate in accordance with 'EU law' and as prescribed by EU directives.

•   It creates another legislature to rival the Queen in Parliament, and enables legislation other than Acts of Parliament to prevail over the Common Law. Such attempts in the past have been found to be unconstitutional. For example, in the *Case of Proclamations* [1610] EWHC KB J22, the Court held it was unlawful for the Crown to legislate by 'proclamations', by-passing Parliament.

• EU law is being made without the consent of the English people: that contravenes the fundamental constitutional principle of ***government by consent.*** .

• EU membership purports to 'transfer' Sovereignty to the EU, or 'share' it with the EU, in breach of the English Constitution whereby Sovereignty is immutably vested in the Queen in Parliament (see *Calvin's* Case (1608) 7 Coke Reports 2a).

• The Treaty on European Union purports to make HM the Queen a 'citizen' of the EU, and "*subject to the duties imposed thereby*". [10] Similarly, all the Queen's subjects are made 'EU citizens' without their consent. That is illegal under the common law.

• By signing the EU Treaties, the responsible Ministers committed High Treason, and breached the Privy Council oath of allegiance, to "*assist and defend all Jurisdictions, Pre-eminences, and Authorities, granted to Her Majesty, and annexed to the Crown... against all Foreign Princes, Persons, Prelates, States, or Potentates*". Their acts were criminal, and therefore void in law.

This fictitious 'marriage' does not require a divorce, amicable or otherwise. As a matter of law, it can be, must be, declared null and void.

---

[10] *Article 8, 2 of the Treaty on European Union, 1992*

5. Historic precedents

There have been many similar unions in history before the European Union. All of them eventually collapsed; and before collapsing, some of them tried to play exactly the same trick. They passed laws, similar to Article 50, introducing a complex and onerous procedure for withdrawal. As a rule, the discontented 'member-states' would then cheerfully ignore the procedure and make unilateral declarations of independence. Their former imperial masters, and the rest of the world, always had to go along with that. Most of the independent states which exist in the world today have had precisely that genesis.

5.1. Collapse of the Soviet Union

It is now becoming less and less controversial to compare the European Union with the old Soviet Union. So far as the author could ascertain, that comparison was first made in secret discussions between Presidents Gorbachev and Mitterrand in 1989-1990 about their plan for a 'common European home'; and at that instance, the comparison was meant as a mutual compliment.

Publicly, the comparison was first drawn by the great Soviet dissident Vladimir Bukovsky in 2002, who observed "with growing horror" that the totalitarian monster he had fought against all his life was suddenly rising from the dead in the form of yet another 'Union'. Some considered it as an exaggeration at the time, but as the years go by the comparison has been becoming more and more apparent, and it is now almost commonplace. There are still Europhiles who are outraged by it, but the controversy is dying down.

At the moment, however, we are concerned with merely one aspect of each Union, namely their legal and constitutional forms, and here the parallels are obvious. Both claimed to be voluntary unions of free nations flourishing under respective Treaties; both, in reality, were something more than that. Even if the substance was, to a degree, different, the structure was similar. Therefore, we would be entirely justified in turning to the experience of the collapse of the USSR to try and draw some lessons for the forthcoming collapse of the EU.

Like the European Constitution (now known under its modest alias the Lisbon Treaty) which provides for a withdrawal from the Union in **Article 50**, the Soviet Constitution had an analogous provision in **Article 72**, which declared each republic's right to withdraw from the Union; additionally, on 3rd April 1990 the Supreme Soviet passed the law '*On the procedure for resolution of issues in connection with a withdrawal of a Union republic from the USSR*'. In summary, the procedure was as follows:

• Following a referendum, the Supreme Soviet of a Republic ('member-state') would notify the Supreme Soviet of the Union, who would then refer the matter to the Congress of People's Deputies.

• The Congress of People's Deputies would then establish a transitional period of no longer than 5 years "to resolve the issues arising in connection with the withdrawal of the Republic from the USSR".

• The Union Constitution and the Union law would remain in force in the withdrawing Republic throughout the transitional period.

Within two years, all 15 Soviet Republics had withdrawn from the Union. **Out of those 15, none followed the procedure**. Instead, each republic had its parliament passing a series of unilateral declarations on unconditional withdrawal, sovereignty, and independence. The leaders of the Union objected most vociferously; their favourite phrase to describe (and demand) adherence to the correct procedure was *"amicable divorce"*.

They appealed to the principle of the rule of law. That failing, they threatened economic blockade. Failing that, they attempted armed coups to depose the withdrawalist leaders. None of that worked however. Sooner than the first application for withdrawal in accordance with Article 72 was made, all 15 republics were independent, and the Union was no more.

Indeed, as in the case of the EU, the detailed procedure was introduced some time after the process of collapse had already began, and a number of republics were already in the process of unilateral withdrawal.

Consider the example of **Lithuania**, annexed by the Soviet Union in 1940. Its parliament (Sejm) then passed a law analogous to our European Communities Act: the republic lost its sovereignty and became the Lithuanian Soviet Socialist Republic (LSSR), with a Supreme Soviet instead of parliament.

In 1989-1990, Lithuanian independence was restored by the following unilateral Acts of the LSSR Supreme Soviet:

• 18th May 1989: the Supreme Soviet enacted that only such laws that had been enacted or ratified by the Lithuanian Supreme Soviet were valid on Lithuanian territory. The Union law no longer had supremacy or direct effect.

• 8th February 1990: the Supreme Soviet declared and enacted that the 1940 acts on accession to the Union were unconstitutional and legally void.

• 11th March 1990: Act of Restoration of the independence of Lithuania.

Lithuania passed those acts unilaterally and unconditionally. In doing so, the Lithuanian parliament consciously breached the USSR Constitution. Moscow denounced those unilateral acts as legally void. Moscow cut oil supplies in an attempt to stifle Lithuania by an economic blockade; that lasted for less than a year and proved ineffective. Moscow attempted an armed coup in Lithuania in January 1991, killing 16 unarmed civilians - that coup failed, too.

The constitutional situation was very similar in **Estonia**; and so was the solution. Here is the summary chronology of Estonia's withdrawal from the USSR by unilateral parliamentary acts:

- **16th November 1988:** Declaration of Sovereignty of Estonia.

- **12th November 1989:** The Estonian Parliament passed an Act 'on the historical and legal assessment of the events in Estonia in 1940': it enacted that the Estonia Parliament's 1940 Act on joining the Soviet Union (analogous to our EEC Act 1973) was declared illegal and void.

- **30th March 1990:** Declaration on the status of Estonia: confirmed that the de jure existence of Estonia as an independent state was not interrupted by the unlawful annexation in 1940; that the state authorities of Estonian SSR were unlawful since their establishment; and declared the restoration of the Estonian Republic.

- **9 May 1990:** Act renaming the Estonian Soviet Socialist Republic as the Estonian Republic.

- **12 January 1991:** Estonia signed a Treaty on international relations with Russian Soviet Federative Socialist Republic whereby (in defiance of the USSR Constitution) both sides recognised each other as sovereign states.

- **20th August 1991:** Resolution 'On state independence of Estonia'.

So the independence of Estonia was restored by a series of unilateral and unconditional acts, in defiance of the USSR's constitution and the Soviet procedure for withdrawal, and despite the USSR refusing to recognise the validity of the Estonian unilateral acts.

Latvia likewise withdrew from the USSR by a unilateral and unconditional act of its own national parliament: Declaration on the restoration of independence of the Latvian Republic on 3rd May 1990.

On 31st March 1991, **Georgia** carried out a referendum on independence from the USSR, where 98.9% voted for independence. On 9th April, the Georgian Supreme Soviet passed the Act on the restoration of state independence of Georgia. The country had been part of the Soviet Union for **70 years**. The 'legal' procedure for withdrawal would have taken **5 years**. The actual process of unconditional withdrawal took **9 days**.

Despite the demands from Moscow, supported by practically the whole world (remember President Bush's 'Chicken Kiev speech', for example), none of those newly independent nations had to come to an agreement with Moscow before a withdrawal. They did it unilaterally; then Moscow and the world came to them **asking** for all sorts of international agreements.

Those nations carried out an unconditional withdrawal; then (very promptly) they naturally recognised each other; and then, also fairly quickly and easily, they came to terms with their former empire and the rest of the world. What could the Union do except accept the *fait accompli*? But had those nations taken a different course, the course now proposed for our withdrawal from the EU, in all likelihood they would be still be negotiating with Moscow to this day.

5.2. EU Treaties: honoured more in breach than in observance

Britain's unconditional withdrawal from the EU would be legal under the English Constitution, but yes, it would be a breach of the Lisbon Treaty. That may sound uncomfortable;

but it would not be the first time where a member state breaches an EU treaty. In every such case, the EU Commission opens an 'infringement case' against the offending member-state. Its 2012 annual report parades the recent successes in the enforcement of the treaties: "*At the end of 2012, 1,343 infringement cases were open. The number of open infringement cases has continued to fall - from nearly 2,900 cases in 2009, to 2,100 cases in 2010 and to 1,775 cases in 2011.*" Then there is a breakdown country by country: from the modest 20 infringement cases against the law-abiding Latvians, to 61 against the rebellious Brits, to 99 against the anarchical Italians. [11] Note these are only the cases which are currently active; the historic numbers will be many times higher.

Every EU member-state breaks the EU treaties all the time; and the worst that happens to them is that the Commission takes them to the European Court of Justice, who may then order them to pay a fine. This has happened to us many times while we have been members of the EU, and it has happened many times to every other member of the EU. If we breached the treaties quite happily as members, why should we suddenly be so careful about strictly following the procedure for leaving the EU?

The worst that can happen to us is an ECJ fine we may now, finally, ignore. Moreover, the entire EU, along with its Commissions and Courts, procedures and fines, may well be on the way to collapse; only time will tell. It makes no sense at all to suddenly observe their procedures on just this occasion – when we need to breach it more than we ever did, and can get away with it more easily than we ever could before.

---

[11] *30th Annual Report on monitoring the application of EU law. Report from the sCommission. General Secretariat, 2012*

6. The exit plan

It is sometimes assumed that an immediate and unilateral withdrawal from the EU would (a) leave huge gaps in our law in place of the abolished EU regulations, leading to chaos and anarchy, and (b) ruin all international co-operation we have developed with the countries of Europe, so that we have to start from scratch.

Both these assumptions are wrong. There was life in Europe, and in Britain, even before the EU; consequently, there is a 'safety net' of pre-EU arrangements, both domestic and international, we can safely 'fall back' on. Of course, some transitional period will be necessary, as discussed below; but in many areas, the transition will be fairly simple and may be completed as a matter of a few months, if not weeks.

Below, we look at the areas where it has been said that the transition would be problematic, only to discover that there is little to fear. Moreover, even where transition appears more complicated, it is evident that it would be sorted out more easily under British control rather than European.

6.1. The Economy and trade

From listening to the ensuing pro-EU scaremongering campaign, one may get the impression that on the day of our withdrawal, trade with each of the 27 other EU member states would immediately cease, until and unless we negotiate some new trade treaties. This is the reverse of the truth. Nations were trading with each other for thousands of years, long before they began to make treaties; and in the modern world, global trade has become increasingly liberalised.

It is not just that there are in place fairly liberal rules of the World Trade Organisation which are binding upon all its members, and it would be against those binding rules for the EU to introduce discriminatory barriers to trade with us.

Trade barriers do not grow on national borders of natural causes; they must be introduced (or not) by governments. Does anyone seriously believe that, if we leave the EU tomorrow, the EU, or any of its member states, would introduce protectionist measures against us? Conventional economic thinking today says that Protectionism is considered detrimental; but even before this liberal age, nobody ever introduced trade barriers against a country with whom they had a trade surplus, as the EU has with us. We have a trade deficit with the EU, in other words, they sell us much more than we sell them.

Therefore, were it in anyone's interest to restrict UK-EU trade, then it would be in ours; and yet this unthinkable idea, which has never been deployed by any serious British withdrawalist, has nevertheless succeeded in becoming the biggest weapon in the pro-EU brigades' propaganda arsenal. Whatever limited success that propaganda weapon has had, it owes to the popular fear of jeopardising trade. Imagine how much more frightening that idea sounds across the Channel, where it would threaten a trade surplus and not a trade deficit!

The EU has perfectly sound free trade agreements, with no political strings attached, with countries like South Korea, Israel or Mexico. There is no reason why a similar agreement cannot be made with the UK. It is true that free trade agreements sometimes take a long time to negotiate, but this is only because when trade is liberalised it may take a long time to identify and remove various rules and procedures in both sides' legal systems that may inadvertently work as 'non-tariff barriers' to trade. No such problems are likely to arise between the EU and the UK, where free trade has been going on for years and a new treaty would simply codify the status quo.

But what if the EU decides to punish us with trade sanctions for undermining its ideological project; like the Soviet Union unsuccessfully tried to do against Lithuania? This is something they cannot do, for two essential reasons. Firstly, any discriminatory measures against us would be an outright breach of the binding rules of the World Trade Organisation; and secondly, the EU simply cannot afford to sacrifice its economic interests to ideology on such a massive scale, especially not when its own economy is in such a desperate state as it is now.

In fact, this is another reason why we should withdraw promptly, when any such 'trade war' is out of the question, rather than spend years and years on negotiations which would either fail completely or end in our capitulation. If there is any risk of a 'trade war' (and I think there is not), now is exactly the time when it is at its lowest and our negotiating position is strongest.

But even in the worst-case scenario, if we fail to negotiate a replacement agreement on free trade, all that will happen is that we 'fall back' on the fairly liberal rules of the World Trade Organisation. An estimated 44% of all imported industrial products, receive duty-free treatment in all developed countries; there is practically a *global* common market now.

Overall, the average tariff on industrial products in developed countries is just 3.8%. [13] Additionally, if it is a real 'trade war' and the EU is determined to do their worst, they can re-introduce physical inspections and document checks for goods imported from Britain, which would of course slow down the flow of trade. [14]

So, while in reality a 'trade war' is highly unlikely, in theory it is true that the EU can punish our exporters with some additional bureaucratic idiocies entailing additional costs. Yet, these potential inconveniences must be balanced against the estimated cost of the EU to our national economy, currently estimated at about **11%** of **GDP**, some **£165** to **£170 billion** p.a., [15] and the benefits from removing the EU's 'common' trade barriers against the rest of the world.

Even so, it would be madness for the EU to put such inconvenient bureaucratic constraints in place against Britain because similar arrangements could be put in place for their exports into the UK, which would be a disaster for their member states given their level of trade with the UK.

Another myth is that, because the EU's 'internal market' is subject to hundreds of EU regulations, setting various standards for goods and services, all those regulations cannot be cancelled overnight because that would cause chaos. To understand the falsity of this argument we only need to think about how this works with our other foreign trading partners. For example, many UK businesses trade with the United States, be that in goods, services, or capital. They know US standards and of course comply with them, otherwise they would not be able to sell their products there. They don't need US standards to be binding in law in the UK in order to do that. Many others trade with India and comply with Indian standards, without any need for those standards to be enshrined in UK law. These markets simply regulate themselves.

Similarly, if Parliament repeals all EU regulations overnight, nothing will change for those UK businesses who trade with the EU. They would still comply with EU standards, not because they are forced to, but because that is their market. At the same time, about **90%** of the UK economy that does not trade with the EU would be immediately freed from the unnecessary burden of countless irrelevant regulations.

There are, of course, larger misconceptions underlying the myth of EU regulations being vital for economy and trade. As William, Earl of Dartmouth, points out [16], a 'regional trade bloc' is not such a natural idea as it may seem. There is no reason

---

[13] *Ibid*

[14] *Richard North, p. 41*

[15] *Congdon, op ed., p. 6*

[16] *William Dartmouth (2014). Out of the EU and into the World. Pp. 59-61*

why trade with geographical neighbours is more important to a country than trade with the rest of the world. On the contrary, throughout the centuries, the very idea of trade was associated first and foremost with faraway travel and remote lands, despite the fact that means of transport were much more restricted and ineffective, and travel much more dangerous, than it is now.

All great trading empires in history, including the greatest of them, which was the British Empire, had their possessions scattered all over the globe (in contrast to empires of a different kind, held together by military power). This is natural: different parts of the world produce different goods, and that is why trade is necessary. But what would geographical neighbours with pretty similar economies sell to each other? Why would they need a trade bloc between themselves? What would be its likely result, except over-regulation by some supranational bureaucracy?

The economy of the EU overall is underperforming in relation to those developed, and developing, economies of nations outside the EU. In the 20 years of the 'Single Market', EU growth has been half to three-quarters of a per cent per annum slower than in the advanced economies of the world as a whole. The IMF expects the gap to widen in the next few years. [17] Why should we tie ourselves to that stultifying bureaucratic economy with its endemic corruption, waste, and inefficiency?

6.2. Justice and Home Affairs

The EU is creating its own system of criminal law known under the misnomer of an area of 'Freedom, Security and Justice'. In fact no descriptor could be further from reality. This is being done by the creation of various legal institutions and instruments which are alien to the English Common Law.

The most significant of these instruments, so far, is the **European Arrest Warrant**, which has caused many notorious cases of gross injustice. That is the EU's replacement of traditional extradition treaties, with their time-tested safeguards for the accused. Under the EAW however, UK citizens are surrendered to other EU member states simply on the force of a piece of paper, whether or not there is any *prima facie* case against them, and with few questions asked.

The EU principles of 'mutual trust' and 'mutual recognition' require that a judicial or prosecutorial decision taken in one EU member-state should be enforced automatically in any other EU member-state. The European Arrest Warrant is the most infamous of the EU 'mutual recognition' instruments. Others extend the same principle beyond arrest warrants to criminal sentences, fines and penalties, searches, interrogations, probation, bail (European Supervision Order), confiscation orders, freezing of assets, etc. Mutual recognition effectively means that **every ex-communist prosecutor or judge in an East European state run by a local mafia is given an equal standing to the judges in the Old Bailey**. This is self-evidently absurd.

At the same time, the alleged benefits of the EAW for the UK are almost entirely illusory. Firstly, it is said that EAW allows the UK to secure the extradition of criminals who would otherwise be safe abroad. Several cases of notorious terrorists or paedophiles extradited to the UK are normally cited in support of this proposition. In fact, there can be no doubt that all these criminals would have been extradited to the UK without the EAW, on traditional extradition requests, just as efficiently.

This is because UK prosecutors only ever issue an EAW or an extradition requests when they are 'trial-ready'. There would be no practical difficulty in presenting the *prima facie* case to a foreign court before extradition, since exactly the same evidence would have to be presented to the UK court, and satisfy more stringent legal and procedural requirements, immediately after

---

[17] Congdon, Tim (2013). How Much Does the EU Cost Britain?. London: self-published by Professor Congdon

the extradition. In reality, the only benefit of replacing outgoing extradition requests with EAWs consists in saving the costs of translation. This is a very cheap price for sacrificing the sacred and ancient constitutional liberties such as *habeas corpus*.

Secondly, it is said that EAW has brought simplicity and speed into extradition proceedings in UK courts. We would answer this by quoting the High Court judgement of Lord Justice Smith and Mr. Justice Irwin in the case of *Regina (Hilali) v Governor of Whitemoor Prison and another [2007] EWHC 939 (Admin)*, para 33:

I accept without hesitation or reserve all that Mr Perry urged upon us about the need for simplicity and expedition in dealing with the execution of EAWs. We would say, in parenthesis, that **anyone who is familiar with the jurisprudence which has developed under Part 1 of the Act would be bound to observe that it has not succeeded in providing a simple and speedy process.** [emphasis added]

At the same time, an abolition of the EAW would cause no practical problems: we would simply 'fall back' on the Council of Europe Convention on Extradition, which still governs our extradition arrangements with a number of countries outside of the EU, while all EU member-states remain its participants. Germany did that, albeit temporarily, when its Constitutional Court suspended the German law on EAW as unconstitutional.

The Convention, however, does not include a mandatory requirement of presenting a *prima facie* case against the accused, which has been the most important safeguard to liberty in our extradition treaties for centuries. However, the signatories can reserve the right to require prima facie case to be presented, and six participants (Andorra, Denmark, Iceland, Israel, Malta and Norway) have made such a reservation.

Unfortunately, at the time UK joined the Convention in 1990, the Tory Government failed to make a similar reservation, and extradition without a prima facie case remains possible. This will need to be re-negotiated. In the meantime, under the Convention (unlike in EAW cases) the Home Secretary will be able to veto any extradition request that does not satisfy the *prima facie* case requirement.

Other 'mutual recognition' instruments can be adequately replaced by restoring the system of mutual legal assistance (MLA). There is an extensive network of international treaties on MLA, most notably the Council of Europe Convention on Mutual Legal Assistance. Not only would it adequately replace the 'mutual recognition' system, but also would allow us to retain the benefits of data-sharing, with adequate data protection safeguards, on a case-by-case basis after opting out of EU databases.

As experience shows, data-sharing and other forms of international co-operation in this area are best organized on a case-by-case administrative basis. Undoubtedly, one of the most successful examples of international co-operation in combating crime is Interpol (notwithstanding all its imperfections). Interpol began as, and largely remains, merely an informal club of senior police officers, and in practice this form of co-operation has proven to be the most flexible and efficient.

So, far from undermining international co-operation in the fight against crime, the withdrawal from the EU will only make it more flexible and efficient. The European Arrest Warrant will be replaced by the already existing framework of more traditional extradition treaties with the appropriate safeguards. Mutual recognition will be replaced with mutual legal assistance. The functions of Europol, Eurojust and other EU institutions can be largely taken over by Interpol. Of course, some improvements will be necessary to bring that system up to date; but on the whole, the alternative system is already in place, and is quite effective in facilitating international co-operation in this area outside the EU.

6.3. Immigration

Various Articles of the Treaty of the Functioning of the European Union give every EU citizen the right to come to Britain if they wish . [18] They also get access to public services, benefits and housing by right on the same basis as British citizens. The same rights are extended to family members of EU citizens even if they are not EU citizens themselves. All these people must be treated in the UK as if they were UK citizens: any 'direct or indirect discrimination' is prohibited.

These are their rights under the EU Treaties. Hundreds of thousands of EU citizens have taken advantage of those rights and settled in the UK. The 2004 expansion of the Union has resulted in massive waves of migration. These waves are continual, depending on the economic circumstances of member states, and as new countries join.

Is this irreversible? Can Britain restore control over its borders and immigration policy, and resolve the crisis? We all know that to have any hope of doing that we have to leave the EU. However, what fewer people realise is that the answer to this question also depends on *how* we withdraw. There is of course no solution to our immigration problems within the EU, but there is also no solution within the 'Article 50 withdrawal' scenario either.

Under EU law, as explained above, the 'vested rights' of EU citizens cannot simply be taken away from them by a member-state; not even if it withdraws from the Union. The UK government can withdraw from its Treaties with other governments, but not from its obligations owed to 500 million EU citizens. All their 'vested rights' will be preserved as 'part of their legal heritage'.

All EU immigrants already in the UK will preserve their right to stay here. It is not unlikely that all other EU citizens and their families will preserve 'vested rights' to come here. But even if

---

[18] TFEU. Articles 21(1), Article 45, Article 49, and Articles 56 & 57

they don't, untold thousands of EU citizens will rush here in advance of the 'negotiated withdrawal' to secure their part of the 'legal heritage' before it is too late. We would be left, perhaps, with a problem similar to those of Ukraine and Baltic states, with their large Russian populations left behind by the Soviet Union.

The EU Council is legally bound to insist on the preservation of 'vested rights' as a non-negotiable part of any 'withdrawal agreement' under Article 50. Given the complexity of the problem, the British government on the other side of the negotiating table will eventually have to agree to a 'Norwegian' model, or some other model, which includes the 'free movement of people'. Whatever other advantages of such a 'withdrawal', we would have to leave our doors wide open to immigration. Otherwise, there can be no agreement, and we are back to the same choice: either full EU membership or unconditional withdrawal.

Of course, the future of EU immigrants in this country is a very difficult and sensitive problem in itself, quite apart from the complexities of EU law. We cannot just turn all of them into illegal immigrants overnight. But when Britain leaves the EU the EU citizens already here would need to have a legal basis for doing so, just as any foreign national does. Like most things constructed by the EU, the free movement of people was meant to be a Gordian Knot of a problem that cannot be unravelled later.

We suggest the following solution. EU citizens resident in the UK should be required to register their presence. Those working, paying taxes, with contractual and family obligations, and with no criminal record, could be given work permits, or the legal right to permanently remain. They would be eligible to apply for citizenship by the usual process in the due course of time.

Those EU citizens who have never worked, lived on benefits, have never paid taxes, or have criminal records, should be required to leave. This would have to be done on a case by case basis, and while we do not underestimate the difficulty we equally cannot accept that non-citizens should have an automatic right to live here on the same basis as citizens. To do so would render British 'citizenship' meaningless.

This can be legally done by an Act of Parliament, but only if our withdrawal from the EU is unconditional and complete. The principle of 'vested rights' is too fundamental to EU law to avoid it. If any elements of EU law remain part of our law (as they inevitably would under any 'withdrawal agreement') that would, arguably, include the 'vested rights' of EU citizens to stay here. 'Arguably' means a lot in this context: it means that our courts will be swamped with hundreds of thousands of lawsuits from EU immigrants challenging every decision which violates their 'vested rights'; and indeed many such lawsuits may be successful. Our own courts may well tell us that it is unlawful to send EU immigrants back home – even criminals, just as we are now not allowed to deny them entry.

To prevent that, withdrawal must be effected by an Act of Parliament which makes its intention perfectly clear and unambiguous. It must repudiate the EU Treaties, and the totality of 'EU law', down to the last jot and tittle. Indeed, it must denounce those Treaties as having been unconstitutional, and therefore null and void, in the first place.

The measures we have to take to sort out the immigration crisis should be reasonable and fair; but even so, they will be legally dramatic, taking away 'legal rights' from millions of people. Under our Constitution, only Parliament can do such a thing; and before doing that, it must very clearly reassert its constitutional authority. A conditional withdrawal would only complicate the constitutional position, and any ambiguity in this matter would prove fatal.

6.4. The Environment

The EU's ideologically motivated targets for climate change have resulted in the disastrous UK **Climate Change Act 2008**. If fully implemented, this Act will result in the return of the British economy to pre-industrial-revolution conditions. Not forgetting of course that the countryside and coastline is being relentlessly cluttered with hideous and useless wind-turbines, which do not work during the 70 per cent of the time the wind does not blow, and which need conventional power station back-up in any case.

The only benefit of wind-farms is to enrich landowners and the companies that build them; but as an EU member we are bound by the EU's environmental legislation. Professor Congdon credibly estimates that the cost of EU regulation to our economy, in the field of renewable energy alone, is **between £28 and £36 billions per annum** (1.75% to 2.25 % of GDP). [19]

Even more importantly for the present debate, the EU carries the green banner of its environmentalist ideology far beyond its own borders. Under their respective arrangements with the EU, Switzerland, Norway, and other EEA countries, have to accept large parts of the EU's environmental agenda. But it goes further than that: as explained above, the EU has applied economic pressure to remote countries from Mongolia to Bolivia to ratify and observe (among other things) the Kyoto Protocol and six other international 'green' conventions as a pre-condition of their admittance into its 'GSP Plus' scheme of trade preferences.

The EU's foreign policy is aimed at an aggressive imposition of the 'green' agenda all over the world. There is hardly any

[19] P.p. 18-19

doubt that they would try to include as much of it as possible into a potential Article 50 'withdrawal agreement' in the UK.

This is not a place for a substantive debate about alleged man-made climate change. Whoever is right or wrong in that debate, one thing that is certain and that is that the UK is perfectly capable of taking care of its own environmental policy. We don't need the EU to decide it for us; especially on ideological and not pragmatic grounds. Unless we withdraw from the EU unconditionally, we will not be in a position to determine a policy that is in our own interests.

6.5. Defence and Foreign Affairs

The Lisbon Treaty makes provision for a Common Foreign and Security Policy, and the EU now has its own foreign minister in the form of Baroness Ashton. This policy is also designed to lead to a 'common defence'. Common armed forces are being created gradually by means of common procurement practices, common command and control structures, and common communications systems. The intent is to ensure that the member states' armed forces (those that have them worthy of the name) cannot, in the course of time, operate independently. Under the Lisbon Treaty's Common External Action Force, member states' diplomatic and embassy functions will also be taken over by the EU.

Leaving the EU would open up a whole range of strategic foreign policy possibilities for Britain. This would enable a much needed root and branch reassessment of what our strategic needs and capabilities are, unencumbered by out-dated historical assumptions and the EU's supranational pretensions. We could put our genuine 'national interest' at the centre of our long-term foreign policy and defence requirement decision making, perhaps for the first time in half a century.

We could continue discussing a whole range of policy areas that are now under the control of the European Union, and the difficulties of extracting ourselves from the EU's legislation. Since most areas of domestic policy have been surrendered to the EU over the last forty years no one can deny that dealing with this legacy will present a big challenge to any British government that decides to leave the EU. But as we have shown above it can be overcome, even in the most complex areas. The most foolish thing that can be done would be to tie the hands of a future government by imposing on it some convoluted and dishonest process of conditional withdrawal.

7. The transitional period

EU withdrawal, at least a genuine withdrawal, means a historic turning point, and a radical change. We say that change would be for the better; our opponents say it would be a change for the worse, and indeed a disaster. There is no point in arguing that nothing will change, or in trying to invent such a clever plan for withdrawal that would only guarantee that nothing substantive would actually change. A timid school of thought has recently emerged among elements of the withdrawalist movement proposing exactly that.

For instance, Dr Richard North has recently published a lengthy and well-researched pamphlet advocating withdrawal through negotiations under Article 50 leading us to a 'Norwegian model' in the EEA. The central argument, as I understand it, is this: *"EEA membership protects Britain's position, more or less guaranteeing that withdrawal would be economically neutral"*. [20] With the estimated cost of EU membership to our economy being in the region of **£165-£170 billion** per annum, an 'economically neutral' withdrawal is the last thing we want. An economically neutral withdrawal whereby we cannot control our own borders, where we have to observe the vested rights of EU citizens, and where we are still saddled with vast areas of EU legislation, would be pointless and we might as well not bother.

Britain's unconditional withdrawal from the EU on the other hand will radically change Britain for the better. But it will also, inevitably, change the EU. The EU's future looks highly uncertain: membership of the euro, over-regulation on business, misguided climate change legislation, are all destroying prosperity and jobs across Europe and chaos and civil disorder has already reared its ugly head.

The withdrawal of Britain, one of the largest net contributors to the EU budget, and the sixth largest economy in the world, may well prove the last straw that breaks the EU's back. If nothing else, many other EU members will be tempted to follow our example.

In any event, it is quite unlikely that the EU has any future in the long term. What we should worry about is not our future relations with the EU, but our future relations with the countries of Europe. National governments at least have to worry about the voters, and will find it much more difficult to sacrifice their economic interests to punish us for ideological reasons.

Why should they hate us for leaving the EU? It is much more likely that they will envy us, if not follow our example. So, when we talk about our 'future relationship' with the EU, that is only a short-term transitional plan; and what we will probably have to deal with is the EU in the process of disintegration.

In these circumstances, negotiations with the EU on withdrawal would be pointless, indeed counterproductive. The EU cannot permit a precedent of a successful withdrawal on beneficial terms, because this might encourage the withdrawal of more Member States. The EU would most likely try to make the negotiations as difficult as possible, ending in the most onerous terms for Britain. These risks are far greater, and far more real, than those of a unilateral withdrawal.

A different question, and perhaps a more difficult one, is how quickly the 'EU legal order' in this country can be dismantled. Constructed over almost half a century, it cannot be removed overnight. We will need time to replace it with new agreements on trade and co-operation with other countries, both inside and outside the EU. Our international trade and, to a large extent, foreign relations have been taken over by Brussels for many years; outside the EU, we will no longer benefit from their international agreements and will have to replace them with our own.

---

[20] P. 48

Furthermore, while a lot of EU legislation can be simply cancelled (to widespread relief), some of it needs to be replaced with national legislation. For example, food safety regulations, or those on dangerous substances, concern areas that we would not want to keep completely de-regulated even for a relatively short period. But the regulation we would enact would be our regulation and not that of the EU.

Finally, the EU system has taken too deep root in British soil to be uprooted overnight. For half a century, an increasing proportion of our laws have been made by the EU and then rubber-stamped by our Parliament. As explained below, many of those laws will remain on the statute book despite the withdrawal, and will need to be repealed and or replaced separately. There is no ready-made list of such laws; a lengthy review will be necessary even to identify all of them, let alone replace them.

It follows that we need a **transitional period** (after unilateral withdrawal) for an orderly withdrawal from EU legislation. In that sense, the two years proposed in the Lisbon Treaty is not unreasonable. The real question is whether the process of withdrawal should be controlled by the EU (as it would happen if it is 'negotiated' under Article 50 of the Lisbon Treaty) or by ourselves (in the event of an unconditional withdrawal). Who is to decide how much of the EU law should stay in force in the transitional period, and for how long?

It is a matter of principle to leave those decisions to our own national government. That in itself makes our position much stronger, even if we voluntarily continue to observe the EU treaties for the entire transitional period; however, such a course would not be advisable. Many disastrous aspects of the EU legal system from uncontrolled immigration, to the European Arrest Warrant must be abolished **urgently**.

It is only relatively small isolated parts of EU law that need a more careful approach. The transitional period must not be used as a smokescreen for delaying our withdrawal. Having voted for withdrawal, be that by a referendum, or by electing a withdrawalist government, the public will expect an immediate action - and quite rightly, too.

7.1. Repeal of the European Communities Act

As soon as the country has spoken in favour of a withdrawal, be that by a referendum or a general election, the government must immediately introduce a Bill repealing the European Communities Act 1972. This would restore the supremacy of national law over EU law, and remove the EU Treaties and legislation from the body of our law.

However, as explained above, a simple repeal would not be sufficient to get rid of all the consequences of the EU 'legal order' and 'vested rights' created by it. It must be firmly established in our law that 'EU law' had been illegal and void from the outset. The principal provisions of the Repeal Act would therefore have to be worded accordingly

While Parliament has a perfect right to pass such an act under the English Constitution, at the international level we will be in breach of the EU Treaty. Yet, the only alternative we have is to observe the EU Treaty but continue being in breach of our own Constitution. Whether we like it or not, that is the choice we face; and if so, observing our own law should come first.

7.2. Negotiations after the withdrawal

The Repeal Act shall reverse the 'incorporation' of EU law into our law. A convenient paradox of our 'dualist' legal system however, is that the EEC/EU Treaties would remain in force as *international treaties* without being any longer part of the law.

No part of the EU law will any longer be enforceable in our courts; but from the Foreign Office point of view, and that of EU member-states, we would remain participants of the treaties, for the time being.

This is a somewhat peculiar legal position, but it is not unheard of. In this particular case, it is quite fortunate for all parties. We will be technically in breach of the Treaty by removing it from our national law; but as explained above, the EU treaties have always been honoured more in the breach than in the observance. The European Commission will be able to sue us for that in the European Court of Justice, and we will happily be able to ignore them.

We will be able to make our own transitional arrangements to complete the withdrawal, retaining such provisions of EU treaties as we consider necessary (an obvious example are those on free trade), for just as long as we consider necessary. The remaining EU member-states will be free to continue dealing with us on the basis of 'free movement of goods, services and capital', after all, that is what both sides want. The flow of free trade will not be interrupted.

What we want to achieve is pretty much what Switzerland is now trying to achieve, and precisely what the EU says must never be allowed to happen. We want to be able to pick and choose such elements of the EU which are to our advantage. We want to preserve the 'common market' but to abolish the 'free movement of people' and other EU ideologically inspired disasters.

The EU has made it very clear, both to Switzerland and to us, that they will not agree to that if they have any choice. Yet, Switzerland has defied them, and unless it now gives in to pressure, the EU will probably have to accept their terms. We should do the same, and by that time at least, we probably won't be fighting the battle alone.

7.3. What happens to the *acquis communitaire*?

EU legislation comes to this country in enormous quantities, and in four forms:
1.   Treaties
2.   Regulations
3.   Directives
4.   Decisions

By virtue of the European Communities Act 1972, Treaties and Regulations apply automatically in the UK as if they were law. The Directives and Decisions do not: they merely oblige the government to 'transpose' them into UK law by enacting separate national legislation. Ever since 1972, the successive Tory and Labour governments have been diligently doing so.

Therefore, most of the *acquis communitaire*, in the form of Directives and Decisions, is now on the UK statute book and not merely on EU statute book. The repeal of the European Communities Act will not remove it automatically; that legislation will have to be reviewed and repealed (possibly with some exceptions) separately by Parliament.

On the other hand, all EU Treaties and Regulations stand or fall by the European Communities Act; once the Act is repealed, the default position is that no EU Treaty or Regulation is any longer in force. Some of them may need to be preserved for the transitional period, until they are replaced with adequate national legislation: for example, food safety regulations or some (carefully selected) environmental regulations (e.g. on carriage of dangerous substances). The reason is that our national law includes no up-to-date rules to 'fall back' on in these areas: thus, the latest comprehensive national legislation on dangerous substances appears to be the Petroleum (Consolidation) Act 1928.[21]

---

[21] *See: Richard North, p.p. 99-100*

This is an issue faced by every nation on establishing, or restoring, its independence: what is to be done with the vast body of law accumulated during the period of foreign government? Thus, India, on leaving the British Empire, 'repatriated' the entire body of its law by Article 372 of its Constitution, which provided that all previous laws remained in force until amended or repealed.

On the other end of the scale are former Soviet republics, which declared all Soviet law null and void and simply started afresh. Our solution will need to lie somewhere in between, but probably closer to the 'Lithuanian' scenario than to the 'Indian' one. After all, to be quite blunt about this, English law in India was an improvement, whereas EU law in Britain was the reverse. Those bits of EU law that are worth preserving, even for a relatively short transitional period, are relatively few, and can be expressly identified.

It is important to have a final deadline, to prevent the transitional period from being prolonged indefinitely, either by deliberate sabotage or by the natural sluggishness of any bureaucracy. It is fair to give the government two years to review the existing EU law and enact such replacements as may be necessary; however, once the people have spoken in favour of a withdrawal, it would be undemocratic to delay that process for longer.

When the EU issued its directives, with deadlines for putting them into effect, the government has always managed to keep those deadlines. There is no reason why the same courtesy should not be extended to the people of the United Kingdom.

7.4. Directives and Decisions

The 'default position' will be different in relation to thousands of EU Directives and Decisions which have already been 'transposed' into UK law, that is to say, dutifully copied and pasted into the ostensibly 'national' legislation.

The original Repeal Act will change their legal status in two important respects:

1.   EU Directives will no longer rank supreme to genuinely national law

2.   We will no longer be obliged to *interpret* national legislation in accordance with EU law and its stated objectives.

Apart from that, however, that legislation will not disappear with the repeal of the European Communities Act. Unlike the provisions of Treaties and Regulations, which will be repealed automatically unless expressly preserved in the Repeal Act, the 'transposed' directives and decisions will remain in force until and unless expressly repealed.

So, the withdrawal will have to be followed by no less than a complete review of all our legislation for nearly 40 years; and that, too, will need to have a fairly tight deadline to ensure that the transitional period does not drag on indefinitely. One might say that such a review, followed by a massive repeal, is long overdue.

Too many times has this country been promised by its successive governments a radical de-regulation in all areas of life, a 'bonfire of unnecessary laws', and a 'Great Repeal Act'. In practice, any changes made were essentially cosmetic, principally because most of the unnecessary laws come from the EU and our own Parliament is powerless to repeal or alter them. It is only a withdrawal from the EU that will finally open the door to restoring our freedom.

8. Conclusion

To sum up, if we follow the Article 50 procedure for a 'negotiated withdrawal', we are unlikely ever to see the United Kingdom restored to an independent self-governing nation:

1. Negotiations will be conducted on behalf of the UK by people of Mr Cameron's ilk who (a) do not want to withdraw and (b) cannot be trusted to protect British national interests.

2. The 2-year period for 'negotiation' under Article 50 can be extended indefinitely, and EU lawyers believe 2 years is "far too short". It is very likely to be extended for much longer, given that all participants are unenthusiastic about withdrawal in the first place.

3. The eventual 'withdrawal agreement' may defer its coming into force, establish a transitional period of any length, and we would still be bound by EU law. In practice, accepting Article 50 means we would most likely be tied to the EU, in one form or another, until its ultimate collapse.

4. A Norwegian-style or Swiss-style arrangement is unacceptable, because we would have to adopt large parts of past and future EU law, including the 'free movement of people', elements of Police and Criminal Justice measures, and also pay contributions to EU budget. Perhaps an improvement, but still in the same maze of 'opt-ins' and 'opt-outs', not true independence.

5. The legal doctrine of 'vested rights' is well-established in EU law. This means that those EU citizens who are already in the UK will preserve their Treaty rights, despite withdrawal; existing

employees will be able to rely on the Social Chapter; etc.; legal opinion is that the Council is obliged under EU law to insist on that as a non-negotiable part of any withdrawal deal.

6.   There is no solution to the problem of **EU immigration** within the Article 50 option.

At the same time, there is no good reason why we cannot or should not ignore Article 50 and withdraw from the EU unilaterally and unconditionally:

7.   From the constitutional law point of view, it is absolutely non-controversial (and has been stated by the Courts in many cases) that Parliament has the legal power to repeal the EEC Act, or to repudiate any international treaty.

8.   Unilateral withdrawal is legal under international law because (a) the Vienna Convention on the Law of Treaties recognises the overriding force of fundamental constitutional provisions of national law, and (b) there is a right to national self-determination, typically given effect by unilateral declarations of independence.

9.   There are many historic precedents for an unconditional withdrawal: for example, the USA in 1776; and all the Soviet republics that declared their independence unilaterally, and successfully defied provisions of the Soviet Constitution analogous to Article 50.

10.   All we need from Europe is free-trade. We will have that without a withdrawal agreement because of (a) economic reasons: given their trade surplus with us; (b) because of World Trade Organisations rules which prohibit discriminatory barriers.

11.   The EU is dying; in the long run, we should think about relations with European nations and not with the artificial political construction that is the European Union.

12.   Of course there needs to be a transitional period for EU legislation enacted into Acts of Parliament; but it should be under British control and not the European Union's.

An unconditional withdrawal from the EU proposed in this pamphlet would mean no less an 'orderly' transition than under Article 50, in fact more orderly; however it will be controlled by our own democratic Parliament and not the EU.

The EU has much to lose from our withdrawal, and nothing to gain; and therefore every incentive to sabotage it.   The worse thing the proponents of EU withdrawal can do now is to lose our nerve and be duped into signing up to the idea of withdrawal by means of Article 50.   We must lead public opinion, and not allow ourselves be led into a trap.

The whole EU construction was intended never to be dismantled; but as Roosevelt said in 1933: "We have nothing to fear but fear itself; nameless, unreasoning, unjustified terror that paralyses needed efforts to turn retreat into advance".

END

Appendix I
'GSP Plus' list of
international conventions

Countries outside the EU are required to ratify and implement the following international conventions as a precondition of obtaining trade preferences under the EU's 'GSP Plus' scheme:

List A: 'conventions relating to core political, human and labour rights':

1.　International Convention on Civil and Political Rights;

2.　International Convention on Economic, Social and Cultural Rights;

3.　International Convention on the Elimination of All Forms of Racial Discrimination;

4.　Convention on the Elimination of All Forms of Discrimination against Women;

5.　Convention against Torture and Other Cruel, Inhuman or Degrading Treatment or Punishment;

6.　Convention on the Rights of the Child;

7.　Convention on the Prevention and Punishment of the Crime of Genocide;

8.　Convention concerning Minimum Age for Admission to Employment (No 138);

9.　Convention concerning the Prohibition and Immediate Action for the Elimination of the Worst Form of Child Labour (No. 182);

10.　Convention concerning the Abolition of Forced Labour (No. 105);

11.　Convention concerning Forced or Compulsory Labour (No. 29);

12.	Convention concerning Equal Remuneration for Men and Women Workers for Work of Equal Value (No. 100);

13.	Convention concerning Discrimination in Respect of Employment and Occupation (No. 111);

14.	Convention concerning Freedom of Association and Protecting of the Right to Organize (No. 87);

15.	Convention concerning the Application of the Principles of the Right to Organize and to Bargain Collectively (No. 98);

16.	International Convention on the Suppression and Punishment of the Crime of Apartheid.

List B: 'conventions relating to the environment, good governance and the fight against drug production and trafficking':

1.	Montreal Protocol on Substances that Deplete the Ozone Layer;

2.	Basel Convention on the Control of Transboundary Movement of Hazardous Wastes and Their Disposal;

3.	Stockholm Convention on Persistent Organic Pollutants;

4.	Convention on International Trade in Endangered Species of Wild Fauna and Flora;

5.	Convention on Biological Diversity;

6.	Cartagena Protocol on Biosafety;

7.	The Kyoto Protocol to the United Nations Framework Convention on Climate Change;

8.	United Nations Single Convention on Narcotic Drugs (1961);

9.	United Nations Convention on Psychotropic Substances (1971);

10.	United Nations Convention against Illicit Traffic in Narcotic Drugs and Psychotropic Substances (988);

11.	United Nations Convention against Corruption (Mexico).

About the Author

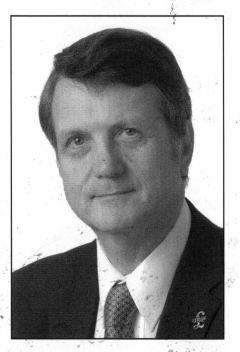

Gerard Batten was first elected to the European Parliament in 2004 for London for the UK Independence Party. He was re-elected in 2009; and elected for a third term in May 2014.

He was a founder member of UKIP in 1993, and has served as a Party Spokesman on Defence and Security, Immigration and Home Affairs. He has written articles, pamphlets, and policy discussion papers on a wide range of subjects.

From 2006 to 2010 he published regular studies on the cost of the European Union to the British economy. In 2011 this work was taken on by Professor Tim Congdon.